90 SOLVED CASES

ON TIME INTELLIGENCE

IN DAX

POWER BI

Business Intelligence

Ramón J. Castro

Introduction by María E. Miranda

When you choose very well where to spend your time,
you have time to do things
that generate value.

Index

Introduction

"90 Solved Cases on Time Intelligence in DAX" is the second of four quick guides to solving cases in the DAX language.

Currently the series includes:

- 180 Solved Cases in Dax Language
  (Published in September 2021)

- 80 Solved Cases on Statistics in Dax
    (to be released)

- 60 Solved Cases on Finance in Dax
    (in press).

Like the previous guide, 90 Solved Cases on Time Intelligence in DAX is a publication for Microsoft Power BI users, this time bringing together 92 IT case studies solved in the DAX language.

All DAX codes collected in this publication can be tested with the "90 Solved Cases on Time Intelligence.pbix" file, which can be downloaded from the following URL:

www.facebook.com/90solvedcasesoftimeintelligenceindax

Time Intelligence in DAX is worked by means of specific Functions that allow the calculation of measurements within periods or time series. By using these Functions, we can see T-SQL queries and the manipulation of large volumes of data within specific time frames greatly simplified.

All Time Intelligence DAX Functions operate on continuous time periods, which makes it essential to have a "Calendar Table" in the model. In cases 1 and 2 of this manual, the code to create such a table is detailed.

001.Create CALENDAR table (1)

Table tools > new table

STEP 1

```
Calendary =
ADDCOLUMNS (
        //start_date, end_date
        CALENDAR ( MIN ( Sales[Date] ), TODAY () ),

        //numeric values
        "year", YEAR ( [Date] ),
        "month", MONTH ( [Date] ),
        "day", DAY ( [Date] ),
        "quarter", QUARTER ( [Date] ),
        "weekDay", WEEKDAY ( [Date] ),
        "weekNum", WEEKNUM ( [Date] ),

        //text values
        "monthName", FORMAT ( [Date], "MMM" ),
        "weekDayName", FORMAT ( [Date], "DDD" ),
        "quarterName", SWITCH ( QUARTER ( [Date] ), 1,
"First", 2, "Second", 3, "Third", 4, "quarter")
)
```

STEP 2

Once the table is finished, it must be marked as a calendar table. To do this we will do the following:

1. Right-click on the table icon.
2. Select the option "Mark as date table".

002.Create CALENDAR table (2)

Table tools > new table

```
Calendary =
//specify the time range of the table
VAR StartDate = Date(2014,1,1)
VAR EndDate = Today()

//create the table
VAR BaseTable = CALENDAR(StartDate, EndDate)

//add YEAR column
VAR Years =
ADDCOLUMNS(BaseTable,"Year",YEAR([Date]) )

//add MONTH column and MONTH-YEAR column
VAR Months =
ADDCOLUMNS(
   Years,
   "Month",MONTH([Date]),
   "Year and Month Number",FORMAT([Date],"YYYY-
MM"),
   "Year and Month Name",FORMAT([Date],"YYYY-MMM")
)

//add QUARTER column and QUARTER-YEAR column
VAR Quarters =
ADDCOLUMNS(
   Months,
   "Quarter",ROUNDUP(MONTH([Date])/3,0),
   "Year and Quarter",[Year] & "-T" &
   ROUNDUP(MONTH([Date])/3,0))

//add DAY, DAY name, DAY number of the YEAR, DAY
number of the WEEK
VAR Days =
ADDCOLUMNS(
```

```
    Quarters,
    "Day",DAY([Date]),
    "Day Name",FORMAT([Date],"DDDD"),
    "Day Of Week",WEEKDAY([Date]),
    "Day Of Year", DATEDIFF (DATE(YEAR([Date]),1,1),
[Date], DAY) + 1)

//add the week number, assuming the week starts on
Sunday
VAR Weeks =
ADDCOLUMNS(
    Days,
    "Week Of Month (Sunday)",INT((DAY([Date])-1)/7)+1,
    "Week of Year (Sunday)",WEEKNUM([Date],1),
    "Year and Week (Sunday)",[Year] & "-W" &
WEEKNUM([Date],1))

//add column: TRUE = from Monday to Friday  /  FALSE =
Saturday and Sunday
VAR WorkingDays =
ADDCOLUMNS(
    Weeks,
    "Is Working Day", NOT WEEKDAY( [Date] ) IN {1,7})

RETURN

WorkingDays
```

STEP 2

Once the table is finished, it must be marked as a calendar table. To do this we will do the following:

1. Right-click on the table icon.
2. Select the option "Mark as date table".

003.Value of a measure between two dates

Modeling > new measurement

```
Sales from 01/05/2014 to 30/05/2015 =
//value of a field within a date range
CALCULATE(
  //expression
  SUM(Sales[ Sales]),
  //filter
  DATESBETWEEN(
    Calendary[Date],
    DATE(2014,05,01),
    DATE(2015,05,30)
  )
)
```

004.List of dates that meet one or more conditions (1)

Table tools > new table

```
Midmarket Summary Sales Date =
//list of dates with Midmarket sales
SUMMARIZE (
  //table or expression returning a table
  CALCULATETABLE (
    //table or expression returning a table
    FILTER ( Sales, Sales[Shipment] ),
    //filter 1, filter 2, filter N,...
    FILTER ( 'Sales', Sales[Sector] = "Midmarket" ),
    FILTER (
      //the function "ALL" does not allow the application
of context filters
      ALL ( 'Sales' ),
      AND (
        Sales[Shipment] >= MIN ( Sales[Shipment] ),
        Sales[Shipment] <= MAX ( Sales[Shipment] )
      )
```

```
    )
  ),
  //columns of the resulting table
  Sales[Sales ID],
  Sales[Shipment]
)
```

005.List of dates that meet one or more conditions (2)
Table tools > new table

```
Orders whithout arrivals dates =
//list of dates with undelivered shipments
SUMMARIZE (
    //table or expression returning a table
    CALCULATETABLE (
        //table or expression returning a table
        Sales,
        //filter 1, filter 2, filter N,...
        FILTER ( 'Sales', Sales[Arrival] = BLANK() )
    ),
    //columns of the resulting table
    Sales[Sales ID],
    Sales[Shipment]
)
```

006.Calculate the latest date based on a condition
Table tools > new table

```
Last Sale by Salesman =
SUMMARIZE(
    //table or expression returning a table
    Sales,
    //group by column
    ROLLUP(Sales[Salesman]),
    //expressions
```

"SaleLastDat", LASTDATE(Sales[Shipment]),
"Ammount",
VAR LDate = MAX(Sales[Sales ID])

RETURN

LOOKUPVALUE(Sales[Sales],Sales[Sales ID],LDate))

007.Calculate the latest date based on more than one condition

Table tools > new table

```
Last Sale > 100K by Salesman on Germany =
SUMMARIZE(
//table or expression returning a table
  CALCULATETABLE(
  //table or expression returning a table
  Sales,
  //filter 1, filter 2, filter N,...
  FILTER(Sales, Sales[Country]="Germany"),
  FILTER(Sales, Sales[ Sales]>100000)
  ),
  ROLLUP(Sales[Salesman]),
  //expression
  "SaleLastDat", LASTDATE(Sales[Shipment]),
  "Ammount",
  VAR LDate =MAX(Sales[Sales ID])
  RETURN
  LOOKUPVALUE(Sales[ Sales],Sales[Sales ID],LDate)
)
```

008.Calculate the penultimate date based on a condition

Table tools > new table

```
Date Previous Sale by Salesman  =
SELECTCOLUMNS(
  //table
  Sales,
  //new column, expression
  "id", Sales[Sales ID],
  "Salesman", Sales[Salesman],
  "prevSales",
  CALCULATE(
      //expression
      LASTDATE(Sales[Shipment]),
      //filter
      FILTER(
        //table or expression returning a table
        Sales,
        //filter
        AND(
          Sales[Salesman] = EARLIER(Sales[Salesman]),
          Sales[Sales ID] < EARLIER(Sales[Sales ID])
        )
      )
  ),
  "Ammount",
  VAR Correct_ID =
  CALCULATE(
      //expression
      MAX(Sales[Sales ID]),
      //filter
      FILTER(
        //table or expression returning a table
        Sales,
        //expression
```

```
        AND(
        Sales[Salesman] = EARLIER(Sales[Salesman]),
        Sales[Sales ID] < EARLIER(Sales[Sales ID])
        )
    )
  )

RETURN

LOOKUPVALUE(Sales[ Sales],Sales[Sales ID], Correct_ID ))
```

009.Calculate penultimate date based on more than one condition

Table tools > new table

```
Date Previous Sale by Salesman with high Discount =
SELECTCOLUMNS(
   //table or expression returning a table
   Sales,
   //column, expression
   "id", Sales[Sales ID],
   "Salesman",Sales[Salesman],
   "Previous sales",
   CALCULATE(
     //expression
     LASTDATE(Sales[Shipment]),
     //filter
     FILTER(
       //table or expression returning a table
       Sales,
       //expression
       AND(
       Sales[Salesman] = EARLIER(Sales[Salesman]),
       Sales[Sales ID] < EARLIER(Sales[Sales ID])
       )
     )
```

```
        ),
            "Ammount",
            VAR Correct_ID =
            CALCULATE(
                //expression
                MAX(Sales[Sales ID]),
                //filter
                FILTER(
                    //table or expression returning a table
                    Sales,
                    //filter
                    AND(
                        Sales[Salesman] = EARLIER(Sales[Salesman]),
                        Sales[Sales ID] < EARLIER(Sales[Sales ID])
                    )
                )
            )

RETURN

//adding conditions to the result using the "IF" function
    IF(
        //condition
        Sales[Discount Band]="High",
        //positive result
        LOOKUPVALUE(
            Sales[ Sales],Sales[Sales ID],
            Correct_ID,
            BLANK())
        )
    )
```

Table tools > new table

```
Last 10 dates with sales over 200K =
TOPN (
  //number of dates
  10,
  //list of last ten dates with sales >200K
  SUMMARIZE (
    //table or expression returning a table
    CALCULATETABLE (
      //table or expression returning a table
      Sales,
      //filter 1, filter 2, filter N,...
      FILTER (
        //table or expression returning a table
        'Sales',
        Sales[ Sales] > 200000
      ),
      FILTER (
        //table or expression returning a table
        'Sales',
        //condition setting the date range
        AND (
          Sales[Shipment] >= MIN ( Sales[Shipment] ),
          Sales[Shipment] <= MAX ( Sales[Shipment] )
        )
      )
    ),
    //columns of the resulting table
    Sales[Sales ID],
    Sales[Shipment],
    Sales[ Sales]
  ),
  Sales[Shipment],
  //from the beginning of the table
```

    DESC
)

011.Get the first N dates that meet one or more conditions (1)
Table tools > new table

First 10 dates with sales over 200K =
TOPN (
    //number of dates
    10,
    //list of last ten dates with sales >200K
    SUMMARIZE (
        //table or expression returning a table
        CALCULATETABLE (
            //table or expression returning a table
            Sales,
            //filter 1, filter 2, filter N,...
            FILTER (
                //table or expression returning a table
                'Sales',
                Sales[Sales] > 200000
            ),
            FILTER (
                //table or expression returning a table
                'Sales',
                //condition setting the date range
                AND (
                    Sales[Shipment] >= MIN (Sales[Shipment]),
                    Sales[Shipment] <= MAX (Sales[Shipment])
)
)
        ),
        //columns of the resulting table
        Sales[Sales ID],
        Sales[Shipment],

```
    Sales[ Sales]
  ),
  Sales[Shipment],
  //starting from the end of the table
  ASC
)
```

012.Get the last N dates that meet one or more conditions (2)

Table tools > new table

```
Last 10 sales over 200K  =
TOPN (
  //number of sales
  10,
  //list of last ten dates with sales >200K
  SUMMARIZE (
    //table or expression returning a table
    CALCULATETABLE (
      //table or expression returning a table
      Sales,
      //filter 1, filter 2, filter N,...
      FILTER ('Sales',
          Sales[ Sales] > 200000
      )
    ),
    //columns of the resulting table
    Sales[Sales ID],
    Sales[Shipment],
    Sales[ Sales]
  ),
  Sales[Sales ID],
  //starting from the end of the table
  DESC )
```

013.Get the first N dates that meet one or more conditions (2)

Table tools > new table

```
Firt 10 sales over 200K  =
TOPN (
  //number of sales
  10,
  //list of last ten dates with sales >200K
  SUMMARIZE (
     //table or expression returning a table
     CALCULATETABLE (
        //table or expression returning a table
        Sales,
        //filter 1, filter 2, filter N,...
        FILTER ('Sales',
             Sales[ Sales] > 200000
           )
     ),
     //columns of the resulting table
     Sales[Sales ID],
     Sales[Shipment],
     Sales[ Sales]
  ),
  Sales[Sales ID],
  //from the beginning of the table
  ASC
)
```

014.Cumulative of a measure in a specific time frame (1)

STEP 1
Modeling > new measurement

Sales last 10 days =

```
CALCULATE (
    //expression
    [Total Sales],
    //filter
    DATESINPERIOD (
        Calendary[Date],
        //find the first context date of each row
        FIRSTDATE ( Calendary[Date] ),
        //numeric value of the period
        -9,
        //time frame (day, month, quarter, year,..
                    )
        DAY
    )
)
```

STEP 2

We take to a table:
Values: 'Calendary'[Date]
Values: [Sales last 10 days]

For each record in the table, it shows the cumulative of the last 10 days.

015.Cumulative of a measure in a specific time frame (2)

STEP 1

Table tools > new table

In this example, the numerical value of the period is variable. For this we are going to create a table containing these values.

Numeric value of the period =

```
//create a table and enter data
//column name ,, field type (INTEGER, DOUBLE, STRING,
BOOLEAN, CURRENCY, DATETIME)
DATATABLE (
    "values", INTEGER,
    //enter data in the fields following the above order

  {
    { 15 },
    { 30 },
    { 45 },
    { 60 },
    { 90 }
  }
)
```

STEP 2

Modeling > new measurement

```
Sales last N days =
CALCULATE (
   //expression
   [Total Sales],
   //filter
   DATESINPERIOD (
      Calendary[Date],
      //find the first context date of each row
      FIRSTDATE ( Calendary[Date] ),
      //numeric value of the period
      SELECTEDVALUE('Numeric value of the
period'[values]),
      //time frame (day, month, quarter, year,..
                )
      DAY
   )
)
```

STEP 3
We take to a table:
Values: 'Calendary'[Date]
Values: [Sales last 10 days]

We take to a slicer:
Value: 'Numeric value of the period'[values]

For each record in the table, it shows the cumulative of the last 10 days.

016.Value of a measure between two dates (1)
Modeling > new measurement

```
Number of order sent last 10 days =
CALCULATE(
    //expression
    COUNTROWS( Sales ),
    //filter
    DATESBETWEEN(
        //table[columnDate]
        Sales[Shipment],
        //oldest date
        TODAY()-10,
        //most recent date
        TODAY()
    )
)
```


017.Value of a measure between two dates (2)
Modeling > new measurement

```
Number of order sent from 25/10/2015 to 25/03/2016 =
CALCULATE(
    //expression
```

```
    COUNTROWS( Sales ),
    //filter
    DATESBETWEEN(
        //table[columnDate]
        Sales[Shipment],
        //oldest date
        DATE(2015,10,25),
        //most recent date
        DATE(2016,03,25)
    )
)
```

018.Calculate the value of a measure from a date to N units of time (1)

Modeling > new measurement

```
Sales last 15 days =
CALCULATE(
  //expression
  SUM(Sales[ Sales]),
  //filter
  DATESINPERIOD(
    //table[columna]
    'Calendary'[Date],
    //base date
    TODAY(),
    //units of time to add or subtract to the base date
    -14,
    //factor (DAY, WEEK, MONTH, QUARTER, YEAR)
    DAY
  )
)
```

Modeling > new measurement

```
Sales last 15 days =
CALCULATE(
   //expression
   [Total Sales],
   //filter
   FILTER(
      //table or expression returning a table
      ALL(Calendary),
      //filter
      AND(
         Calendary[Date]>=TODAY()-15,
         Calendary[Date]<TODAY()
      )
   )
)
```

020.Calculate the value of a measure from the start of each week to the end of the same week

Modeling > new measurement

STEP 1
Table tools > new column

In the Calendary table we create the following column:

```
YearWeek =
CONCATENATE('Calendary'[year],'Calendary'[weekNum])
```

STEP 2
Modeling > new measurement

```
Sales Week to Date =
```

```
VAR CurrentDate =  MIN('Calendary'[Date])
VAR CalYearWeek = MIN('Calendary'[YearWeek])

RETURN
CALCULATE(
   //expression
   [Total Sales],
   //filter
   FILTER (
      //table or expression returning a table
      //function "ALL" does not allow the application of
context filters
      ALL ('Calendar'),
      //filter
      'Calendary'[YearWeek] = CalYearWeek &&
'Calendary'[Date] <= CurrentDate
   )
)
```

021.Calculate the value of a measure from the beginning of the month to the last date of the current context (1)

Modeling > new measurement

```
Current month Sale (1) =
//shows the total sales from the beginning of the month
to the current day.
CALCULATE(
   //expression
   [Total Sales],
   //filter
   DATESMTD(Calendar[Date])
)
```

Calculate the value of a measure from the beginning of the month to the last date of the current context (2)
Modeling > new measurement

Current month sales (2) =
//run an expression from the first day of the CURRENT month until now
//measurement is reset to zero at the beginning of each month
TOTALMTD(
    //expression
    SUM(Sales[Sales]),
    //table [column] of dates
    'Calendary'[Date]
)

023.Calculate the value of a measure from the beginning of the month to the last date of the current context (3)
Modeling > new measurement

Current month sales (3)=
//run an expression from the first day of the CURRENT month until now
//measurement is reset to zero at the beginning of each month
CALCULATE(
    //expression
    SUM(Sales[Sales]),
    //filter
    DATESMTD(Calendary[Date])
)

Modeling > new measurement

STEP 1
Table tools > new column

In the Calendary table we create the following column:

YearMonth =
CONCATENATE('Calendary'[year],'Calendary'[month])

STEP 2
Modeling > new measurement

```
Sales Month to Date (4) =
   VAR CurrentDate = MIN('Calendary'[Date])
   VAR CalYearMonth = MIN('Calendary'[YearMonth])

   RETURN
   CALCULATE(
     //expression
     [Total Sales],
     //filter
     FILTER (
       //table or expression returning a table
       //function "ALL" does not allow the application of
context filters
       ALL ( 'Calendary'),
       'Calendary'[YearMonth] = CalYearMonth &&
'Calendary'[Date] <= CurrentDate
     )  )
```

025.Calculate the value of a measure from the beginning of the quarter to the last date of the current context (1)

Modeling > new measurement

```
Current quarter sales (1) =
CALCULATE(
   //expression
   [Total Sales],
   //filter
   DATESQTD( 'Calendary'[Date] )
)
```

026.Calculate the value of a measure from the beginning of the quarter to the last date of the current context (2)

Modeling > new measurement

```
Current quarter sales (2) =
//runs an expression from the first day of the CURRENT
quarter until now
//measurement is reset to zero at the beginning of each
quarter
TOTALQTD(
  //expression
  SUM(Sales[ Sales]),
  //table [column] of dates
  Calendary[Date]
 )
```

027.Calculate the value of a measure from the beginning of the quarter to the last date of the current context (3)

Modeling > new measurement

Current quarter sales (3)=
//runs an expression from the first day of the CURRENT
quarter until now
//measurement is reset to zero at the beginning of each
quarter
CALCULATE(
   //expression
   SUM(Sales[Sales]),
   //filter
   DATESQTD(Calendary[Date])
)

028.Calculate the value of a measure from the
beginning of the quarter to the last date of the current
context (4)
Modeling > new measurement

STEP 1
Table tools > new column

In the Calendary table we create the following column:

YearQuarter =
CONCATENATE('Calendary'[year],'Calendary'[quarter])

STEP 2
Modeling > new measurement

Sales Quarter to Date (4) =
//create two variables
VAR CurrentDate = MIN('Calendary'[Date])
VAR CalYearQuarter = MIN('Calendary'[YearQuarter])

RETURN

```
CALCULATE(
    //expression
    [Total Sales],
    //filter
    FILTER (
        //table or expression returning a table
        //function "ALL" does not allow the application of
context filters
        ALL ( 'Calendary'),
        //filter
        'Calendary'[YearQuarter] = CalYearQuarter &&
'Calendary'[Date] <= CurrentDate  ) )
```

029.Calculate the value of a measure from the beginning of the year to the last date of the current context (1)

Modeling > new measurement

```
Accumulated sale since the beginning of the year (1) =
CALCULATE(
    //expression
    [Total Sales],
    //filter
    DATESYTD( 'Calendary'[Date] )
)
```

030.Calculate the value of a measure from the beginning of the year to the last date of the current context (2)

Modeling > new measurement

```
Accumulated sale since the beginning of the year (2) =
//execute an expression from the first day of the current
year until now
```

```
//measurement is reset to zero at the beginning of each
year
TOTALYTD(
   //expression
   SUM(Sales[ Sales]),
   //table [column] of dates
   Calendary[Date]
)
```

031.Calculate the value of a measure from the beginning of the year to the last date of the current context (3)

Modeling > new measurement

```
Accumulated sale since the beginning of the year (3) =
//execute an expression from the first day of the current
year until now
//measurement is reset to zero at the beginning of each
year
CALCULATE(
   //expression
   SUM(Sales[ Sales]),
   //filter
   DATESYTD(Calendary[Date])
)
```

032.Calculate the value of a measure from the beginning of the year to the last date of the current context (4)

Modeling > new measurement

```
Accumulated sale since the beginning of the year (4) =
//create two variables
VAR CurrentDate = MIN('Calendary'[Date])
VAR CalYear = MIN('Calendary'[Year])
```

RETURN

```
CALCULATE(
   //expression
   [Total Sales],
   //filter
   FILTER (
      //table or expression returning a table
      //function "ALL" does not allow the application of
context filters
      ALL ( 'Calendary'),
      //filter
      'Calendary'[Year] = CalYear && 'Calendary'[Date] <=
CurrentDate
   )
)
```

033.Calculate the value of a measure at the beginning of the month

Modeling > new measurement

```
Balance at the beginning of the month =
OPENINGBALANCEMONTH(
   //expression
   [Total Sales],
   //table [column] of dates
   Calendary[Date]
)
```

034.Calculate the value of a measure at the beginning of the quarter

Modeling > new measurement

Balance at the beginning of the quarter =

OPENINGBALANCEQUARTER(
    //expression
    [Total Sales],
    //table [column] of dates
    Calendary[Date]
)

035.Calculate the value of a measure at the beginning of the year

Modeling > new measurement

Balance at the beginning of the year =
OPENINGBALANCEYEAR(
    //expression
    [Total Sales],
    //table [column] of dates
    Calendary[Date]
)

036.Calculate the value of a measure at the end of the month

Modeling > new measurement

Balance at the end of the month =
CLOSINGBALANCEMONTH(
    //expression
    [Total Sales],
    //table [column] of dates
    Calendary[Date]
)

037.Calculate the value of a measure at the end of the quarter

Modeling > new measurement

Balance at the end of the quarter =
CLOSINGBALANCEQUARTER(
    //expression
    [Total Sales],
    //table [column] of dates
    Calendary[Date]
)

038.Calculate the value of a measure at the end of the
year
Modeling > new measurement

Balance at the end of the year =
CLOSINGBALANCEYEAR(
    //expression
    [Total Sales],
    //table [column] of dates
    Calendary[Date]
)

039.Calculate the value of a measure corresponding to
a period parallel to the current context
Modeling > new measurement

Last Quarter Sales =
CALCULATE(
    //expression
    [Total Sales],
    //filter
    //values of argument <interval>: MONTH, QUARTER,
YEAR
    PARALLELPERIOD(Calendary[Date],-1,QUARTER)
)

040.Calculate the value of a measure corresponding to the same period of the previous year
Modeling > new measurement

```
Last year sales on same period =
CALCULATE(
   //expression
   [Total Sales],
   //filter
   SAMEPERIODLASTYEAR(Calendary[Date])
)
```

041.Calculate the % in units of time elapsed between two dates and the context of the measurement
Modeling > new measurement

```
Current year (%) =

VAR StartDate =  DATE ( 2021, 01, 01 )
VAR EndDate =    DATE ( 2021, 12, 31 )


RETURN

DIVIDE(
    DATEDIFF( StartDate, TODAY(), DAY),
    DATEDIFF( StartDate, EndDate, DAY)
)
```

NOTE:
Base:
0: US (NASD) 30/360
1: Current/current
2: Current/360
3: Current/365
4: European 30/360

042.Calculate cumulative totals by periods (1)

Modeling > new measurement

```
Sales period acummulated =
CALCULATE(
   //expression
   [Total Sales],
   //filter
   DATESBETWEEN(
     Calendary[Date],
     FIRSTDATE(ALL(Calendary[Date])),
     LASTDATE(Calendary[Date])
   )
)
```

043.Calculate cumulative totals by periods (2)

Modeling > new measurement

```
Sales period acummulated (2) =
CALCULATE(
   //expression
   [Total Sales],
   //filter
   KEEPFILTERS(
     DATESBETWEEN(
       Calendary[Date],
       DATE(2015,06,01),
       DATE(2016,06,30)
     )
   )
)
```

044.Calculate the frequency of a measurement within a time frame

Modeling > new measurement

STEP 1

Table tools > new table

Create the following table.

```
Sales frequency by salesman =
SELECTCOLUMNS(
    //table or expression returning a table
    Salesman,
    //new column, expression
    "Salesman", Salesman[Salesman],
    "First Sale", FIRSTDATE(Calendary[Date]),
    "Last Sales", LASTDATE(Calendary[Date]),
    "Period", DATEDIFF(
                FIRSTDATE(Calendary[Date]),
                LASTDATE(Calendary[Date]),DAY),
    "Sales number", COUNTROWS(RELATEDTABLE(Sales)),
)
```

STEP 2

Table tools > new column

In the table above, create a calculated column with the frequency measure.

```
Sales frequency =
ROUND(
  DIVIDE(
    'Sales frequency by salesman'[Period] ,
    'Sales frequency by salesman'[Sales number]
  ),
  2
)
```

045.Calculate a measure over the current day
Modeling > new measurement

```
Sales today =
//total sales on the day
CALCULATE(
  //expression
  SUM(Sales[ Sales]),
  //filter
  Sales[Date] = TODAY()
)
```

046.Calculate a cumulative measure per day
Modeling > new measurement

```
Accumulated balance per day =
CALCULATE(
  //expression
  [Total Sales],
  //filter
  FILTER(
    //table or expression returning a table
    ALLSELECTED(Calendary[Date]),
    //filter
    Calendary[Date]<=MAX(Calendary[Date])
  )
)
```

047.Calculate the accumulated per unit of time (1)
Table tools > new column

```
CashFlow by Date =
//create a calculated column in the table "Cashflow".
//cash balance value per transaction
CALCULATE (
  //expression
```

```
    SUM ( CashFlow[Movement] ),
    //filter
    FILTER (
        //table or expression returning a table
        CashFlow,
        //filter
        //the EARLIER function allows you to access the value
of a column.
        CashFlow[Date] <= EARLIER ( CashFlow[Date] )
    )
)
```

048.Calculate the accumulated per unit of time (2)
Modeling > new measurement

```
Sales_2016 =
//computation of an expression that is not affected by
context filters
//expression, filter
CALCULATE (
    //expression
    SUM ( Sales[ Sales] ),
    //filter
    FILTER (
        //table or expression returning a table
        //ALL avoids the application of context filters outside
of the calculated expression
        ALL ( Sales ),
        //expression
        //the RELATED function returns a matching row value
between the columns of two related tables
        RELATED ( 'Calendary'[year] ) = 2016
    )
)
```

049.Calculate the accumulated per unit of time (3)
Modeling > new measurement

```
Sales by Year =
 //computation of an expression that is not affected by
context filters
CALCULATE (
   //expression
   SUM ( Sales[ Sales] ),
   FILTER (
      //table or expression returning a table
      //ALL avoids the application of context filters outside
of the calculated expression
      ALL ( Sales ),
      //filter
      Sales[Date] <= MAX(Sales[Date])
   )
)
```

050.Calculate a measure at the beginning of each month
Modeling > new measurement

STEP 1
Modeling > new measurement

```
Accumulated sales =
//create a cumulative measure of sales
CALCULATE(
   //expression
   [Total Sales],
   //filter
   DATESBETWEEN(
      'Calendary'[Date],
      FIRSTDATE(ALL('Calendary'[Date])),
      LASTDATE('Calendary'[Date])
```

)
)

STEP 2
Modeling > new measurement

Displays at the first of each month the cumulative value of a measure. By default, if Power BI does not find a value for the cumulative for the month, it assigns the cumulative total. This always occurs for the first date of the context. We use the conditional so that it assigns the value "0" instead of the cumulative total.

```
Accumulated sale at the beginning of the month =
IF(
  //condition
  AND(FIRSTDATE(Sales[Shipment]),
      [Total Sales]=[Accumulated sales]
  ),
  //positive result
  0,
  //negative result
  OPENINGBALANCEMONTH(
     [Accumulated sales],
     'Calendar'[Date]
  )
)
```


STEP 3
When representing the result in a table or in a chart, you must work with a monthly time frame.

STEP 1
The calendar table must have a column containing the year and another column containing the month.

If this is not the case, we create both columns.

STEP 2
Table tools > new columna

In the calendar table we create a column corresponding to the fiscal year.

```
fiscalYear =
//The variable indicates the last month of the fiscal year.
VAR lastMonth = 3

RETURN
'Calendary'[year] + IF(MONTH('Calendary'[Date]) >
lastMonth, 1, 0)
```


STEP 3
Table tools > new columna

In the calendar table we create a column corresponding to the fiscal month.

```
fiscalMonth =
//The variable indicates the last month of the fiscal year.
VAR lastMonth = 3

RETURN
```

```
//The MOD function returns the remainder of a division.
MOD(MONTH('Calendary'[Date]) - lastMonth, 12) + 1
```

052.Calculate the value of a measure corresponding to a period prior to the current one

Modeling > new measurement

```
Sales last month =
CALCULATE(
    //expression
    [Total Sales],
    //filter
    DATEADD(
        //table[columna]
        Sales[Shipment],
        //number of periods
        -1,
        //timeframe of the period (day, week, month,
quarter, year)
        MONTH
    )
)
```

053.Calculate the time difference between two dates

Table tools > new column

Create a new column in the table "Sales".

```
Days per sent =
//difference of time between two dates
DATEDIFF(
    //most recent date
    Sales[Date2],
    //oldest date
```

    Sales[Date],
    //time unit
    DAY
)

054.Get a date from another date by adding or subtracting months
Table tools > new column

Create a calculated column in the table "Sales".

Indicative delivery time =
EDATE(
    //origin date
    Sales[Shipment],
    //number of positive or negative months from a fixed
numerical value or from the fields of a column
    1
)

055.Get the date corresponding to the last day of the
month from a date
Table tools > new column

Create a calculated column in the "Sales" table

Last day of month =
EOMONTH(
    Sales[Shipment],
    //number of positive months from a fixed numerical
value or from the fields of a column
    //zero value returns the last day of the current month
    0
)

056. Get the date corresponding to the last day of the previous month from a date
Table tools > new column

Create a calculated column in the "Sales" table
Last day of last month =
EOMONTH(
    Sales[Shipment],
    //number of positive months from a fixed numerical value or from the fields of a column
    //negative numeric value returns the last day of the last month
    -1
)

057. Get the last day of the month in the current context
Table tools > new column

STEP 1
Create a calculated column in the table "Sales".

Last day of the month =
ENDOFMONTH(Sales[Shipment])

058. Get the last day of the quarter in the current context
Table tools > new column

STEP 1
Create a calculated column in the table "Sales".

Last day of the quarter =
ENDOFQUARTER(Sales[Shipment])

059.Get the last day of the year in the current context
Table tools > new column

STEP 1
Create a calculated column in the table "Sales".

Last day of the year =
ENDOFYEAR(Sales[Shipment])

060.Get the first day of the month in the current context
Table tools > new column

STEP 1
Create a calculated column in the table "Sales".

First month day =
STARTOFMONTH(Sales[Shipment])

061.Get the first day of the quarter in the current context
Table tools > new column

STEP 1
Create a calculated column in the table "Sales".

First quarter day =
STARTOFQUARTER(Sales[Shipment])

062.Get the first day of the year in the current context
Table tools > new column

STEP 1
Create a calculated column in the table "Sales".

First year day =
STARTOFYEAR(Sales[Shipment])

063.Get the value of a measurement one day later
Modeling > new measurement

Sales next day =
CALCULATE(
   //expression
   [Total Sales],
   //filter
   //returns a column with the date corresponding to the
next day of the current context
   NEXTDAY(Sales[Shipment])
)

064.Get the value of a measure one month later
Modeling > new measurement

Sales next month =
CALCULATE(
   //expression
   [Total Sales],
   //filter
   //returns a column with the date corresponding to the
month following the current context
   NEXTMONTH(Sales[Shipment])
)

065.Get the value of a measure one quarter later
Modeling > new measurement

Sales next quarter =

```
CALCULATE(
    //expression
    [Total Sales],
    //filter
    //returns a column with the date corresponding to the
quarter following the current context
    NEXTQUARTER(Sales[Shipment])
)
```

066.Get the value of a measurement one year later

Modeling > new measurement

```
Sales next year =
CALCULATE(
    //expression
    [Total Sales],
    //filter
    //returns a column with the date corresponding to the
year following the current context
    NEXTYEAR(Sales[Shipment])
)
```

067.Get the value of a measure from the previous day

Modeling > new measurement

```
Sales previous day =
CALCULATE(
    //expression
    [Total Sales],
    //filter
    //returns a column with the date corresponding to the
day before the current context
    PREVIOUSDAY(Sales[Shipment])
)
```

068.Get the value of a measure to the previous month

Modeling > new measurement

```
Sales previous month =
CALCULATE(
    //expression
    [Total Sales],
    //filter
    //returns a column with the date corresponding to the
month preceding the current context
    PREVIOUSMONTH(Sales[Shipment])
)
```

069.Get the value of a measure to the previous quarter

Modeling > new measurement

```
Sales previous quarter =
CALCULATE(
    //expression
    [Total Sales],
    //filter
    //returns a column with the date corresponding to the
date corresponding to the quarter before the current
context
    PREVIOUSQUARTER(Sales[Shipment])
)
```

070.Get the value of a measure from the previous year

Modeling > new measurement

```
Sales previous year =
CALCULATE(
    //expression
```

    [Total Sales],
    //filter
    //returns a column with the date corresponding to the
date corresponding to the year before the current context
    PREVIOUSYEAR(Sales[Shipment])
)

STEP 1
Table tools > new column

In the Calendary table we create the following column:

YearWeek =
CONCATENATE('Calendar'[year],'Calendar'[weekNum])

STEP 2
Modeling > new measurement

Now we create the measure that will perform the calculation.

Total sales same week last year =
    VAR CalendarYear = MIN(Calendar[Year]) - 1
    VAR CalendarWeek = MIN(Calendar[weekNum])
    VAR CalYearWeek =
      IF (
        //condition
        CalendarWeek < 10,
        //positive result
        CONCATENATE(CalendarYear, CONCATENATE("0",
CalendarWeek)),
        //negative result

```
        CONCATENATE(CalendarYear,CalendarWeek)
    )

  RETURN

    CALCULATE(
        //expression
        [Total Sales],
        //filter
        FILTER (
            //"ALL" does not allow the application of context
filters
            ALL ('Calendar'),
            //create a filter where the current week-year is
equal to the previous week-year.
            'Calendar'[YearWeek] = CalYearWeek
            )
        )
    )
```

Compare current week with previous week

Modeling > new measurement

```
Sales last week =
CALCULATE(
  //expression
  [Total Sales],
  //filter
  FILTER(
    //table or expression returning a table
    ALLSELECTED( Calendary[weekNum] ),
    //filter
    Calendary[weekNum] =
    SELECTEDVALUE( Calendary[weekNum] ) -1
  )
)
```

073.Compare current month with previous month
Modeling > new measurement

```
Sales last month (2) =
CALCULATE(
  //expression
  [Total Sales],
  //filter
  FILTER(
    //table or expression returning a table
    ALLSELECTED( Calendary[month] ),
    //filter
    Calendary[month] =
    SELECTEDVALUE( Calendary[month] ) -1
  )
)
```

074.Compare current quarter with previous quarter
Modeling > new measurement

```
Sales last quarter (2) =
CALCULATE(
  //expression
  [Total Sales],
  //filter
  FILTER(
    //table or expression returning a table
    ALLSELECTED( Calendary[quarter] ),
    //filter
    Calendary[quarter] =
    SELECTEDVALUE( Calendary[quarter] ) -1
  )
)
```

075.Compare current year with previous year
Modeling > new measurement

```
Sales last year (2) =
CALCULATE(
   //expression
   [Total Sales],
   //filter
   FILTER(
      //table or expression returning a table
      ALLSELECTED( Calendary[year] ),
      //filter
      Calendary[year] =
      SELECTEDVALUE( Calendary[year] ) -1
   )
)
```

076.Selection of days as working or non-working days
Table tools > new table

STEP 1
Load or create a table containing the holidays.
In the example, this table is called 'Public Holiday'.

STEP 2
Relate the date fields of the table 'Calendary' and the
table 'Public Holiday'.

STEP 3
Create a new column in the 'Calendary' table.
Table tools > new column

```
Public Holyday =
IF(
```

```
  //condition
  COUNTROWS( RELATEDTABLE('Public Holiday')) = 0,
  //workday
  TRUE(),
  //holiday
  FALSE()
)
```

077.Selection of weekends

Table tools > new column

STEP 1

Create a new column in the 'Calendary' table.
Table tools > new column

```
Weekend day =
IF(
  //condition
  Calendary[weekDay] < 6,
  //Monday to Friday
  TRUE(),
  //saturday, sunday
  FALSE()
)
```

078. Selection of days as working or non-working days and weekends

Table tools > new table

STEP 1

Load or create a table containing holidays, not weekends.
In the example, this table is called 'Public Holiday'.

STEP 2
Relate the date fields of the table 'Calendar' and the table 'Public Holiday'.

STEP 3
Table tools > new column

In the 'Calendar' table we create a new column.

```
Public Holyday and Weekend =
IF(
  AND(
    //condition for holidays
    COUNTROWS( RELATEDTABLE('Public Holiday')) = 0,
    //condition for weekends
    Calendary[weekDay] < 6
  ),
  //workday
  TRUE(),
  //holiday
  FALSE()
)
```

079.Create a table showing the value of a measure for each year/month

STEP 1
Table tools > new column

It is very useful when plotting months with their respective years.
This column will be created inside the "Calendary" table.

```
Year-month =
FORMAT(Calendar[Date], "MM-yy")
```

STEP 2
Table tools > new column

The column must be sorted before plotting.

Month year order =
FORMAT(Calendar[Date], "YYYYMM")

080.Combine year and month in the same column
Table tools > new column

STEP 1
In the Calendary table we create the following column:

YearWeek =
CONCATENATE('Calendar'[year],'Calendar'[weekNum])

081.Convert date with text format to date with datetime format
Modeling > new measurement

From text to datatime =
//date in quotation marks
DATEVALUE("15/11/2021")

NOTE:
The time included in the result is always 00:00:00

082.Convert time with text format to time with datetime format (1)
Table tools > new column

Hour in datatime (1) =
//create calculated column in the table "Calendary".

TIMEVALUE(´Calendary´[Date])

083.Convert time with text format to time with datetime format (2)

Modeling > new measurement

Hour in datatime (2) =
//hour,minutes,seconds
TIMEVALUE("14:40:16")

084.Date and time of the last report update

UTC is the main time standard by which the world regulates clocks and time.

STEP 1
1-Create a single column table in the "Specify Data" option.
2-The name of the table will be "UTCDATE".
3-Click on "Edit".
4-In PowerQuery: Add column > custom column.
5-We call the column "LastUpDate".
6-In the formula box we write:

//the UTC value for Spain is 1
=DateTimeZone.SwitchZone(DateTimeZone.LocalNow(),1,
0)

7-Configure column as type: "Date/Time/Time Zone".
8-Close and apply changes

STEP 2
Take in Power BI the column "LastUpDate" to a card. Every time the report is updated, the date and time of the card

will be updated. This way, users will know when the report was last updated.

085.Current date and time by country

Modeling > new measurement

UTC Spain =
//UTC is the main time standard by which the world regulates clocks and time.
//the value for Spain is +1
UTCNOW() + TIME(1,0,0)

086.Visualize run times on a Gantt chart

Modeling > new measurement

It is taken as an example to visualize in a Timeline chart the transit time elapsed between the shipment of each order and its delivery.

STEP 1
Force a second relationship between the tables "Calendary" and "Sales". To do this, we go to the relationship part of Power BI and drag the "Date" field of the "Calendary" table to the "Arrival" field of the "Sales" table.

STEP 2
Table tools > new table

Shipment Gantt =
SELECTCOLUMNS(
      GENERATE(
            Sales,
            FILTER(

                    Calendary,
                    Calendary[Date]>=
Sales[Shipment]&&Calendary[Date]<=
IF(Sales[Arrival]=BLANK(),TODAY(),Sales[Arrival])
)
        ),

        "Sales_Id", Sales[Sales ID],
        "Date", Calendary[Date]
)

STEP 3
We use a Timeline chart to visualize the result.

087.Calculate a measure over the previous month
Modeling > new measurement

```
Sales last month (3) =
CALCULATE(
   //expression
   [Total Sales],
   //filter
   PREVIOUSMONTH( Sales[Shipment] )
)
```


088.Calculate a measure over the previous quarter
Modeling > new measurement

```
Sales last quarter (3) =
CALCULATE(
   //expression
   [Total Sales],
   //filter
   PREVIOUSQUARTER( Sales[Shipment] ) )
```

089.Calculate a measure over the previous year

Modeling > new measurement

```
Sales last year (3) =
CALCULATE(
   //expression
   [Total Sales],
   //filter
   PREVIOUSYEAR( Sales[Shipment] )
)
```

090.Calculate a measure over the next month

Modeling > new measurement

```
Sales next month (3) =
CALCULATE(
   //expression
   [Total Sales],
   //filter
   NEXTMONTH( Sales[Shipment] )
)
```

091.Calculate a measure over the next quarter

Modeling > new measurement

```
Sales next quarter (3) =
CALCULATE(
   //expression
   [Total Sales],
   //filter
   NEXTQUARTER( Sales[Shipment] )
)
```

Modeling > new measurement

```
Sales next year (3) =
CALCULATE(
    //expression
    [Total Sales],
    //filter
    NEXTYEAR( Sales[Shipment] )
)
```

STARTOFMONTH (060)
STARTOFQUARTER (061)
STARTOFYEAR (062)
TIMEVALUE (082,083)
TODAY (001,016,018,019,041,045,086)
TOTALMTD (022)
TOTALQTD (026)
UTCNOW (085)
WEEKDAY (001,002)
WEEKNUM (001,002)
YEAR (001,002)

www.ingramcontent.com/pod-product-compliance
Lightning Source LLC
Chambersburg PA
CBHW061341120726
48001CB00002B/965